Pagan Portals
Hedge Riding

Pagan Portals
Hedge Riding

Harmonia Saille

Winchester, UK
Washington, USA

First published by Moon Books, 2012
Moon Books is an imprint of John Hunt Publishing Ltd., Laurel House, Station Approach,
Alresford, Hants, SO24 9JH, UK
office1@o-books.net
www.o-books.com

For distributor details and how to order please visit the 'Ordering' section on our website.

Text copyright: Harmonia Saille 2011

ISBN: 978 1 78099 348 5

A CIP catalogue record for this book is available from the British Library.

Design and cover photograph: Stuart Davies

Printed and bound by CPI Group (UK) Ltd, Croydon, CR0 4YY
Printed in the USA by Offset Paperback Mfrs, Inc

We operate a distinctive and ethical publishing philosophy in all
areas of our business, from our global network of authors to
production and worldwide distribution.

CONTENTS

Dedication

For my friends in the Circle of Áine

Acknowledgements

Many, many thanks go to the members of The Circle of Áine, Ireland, particularly Kat and Collette (who are mentioned in some way in this book). Other thanks go to Martin Duffy and everyone at Shamanism Ireland, the Irish Centre for Shamanic Studies.

Introduction

The Hedge Riding Hedge Witch

Many people call themselves hedge witches but the true hedge witch will practice the main feature of hedge witch-craft — hedge riding. However, the individual hedge witch's other interests and practices may vary. Not every hedge witch lives in a rural cottage in the forest or on the edge of the village, many live in the suburbs and in towns with only a window box as a garden. However, this will not stop the determined person, from their daily hedge witchcraft pursuits.

Hedge riding is the journey of your spirit into the other-world realms. These are generally the upper and lower worlds. There is also a middle realm, our everyday world, which has spiritual aspects. We can use this realm to travel back into the past to meet our ancestors, former selves, or forward to the future. In the lower world, an earthy place, you will find your animal guides and it also has access to the underworld of the souls of the dead. In the upper world is the home of the divine, gods and goddesses, spirit guides and wise teachers. Having said this, to otherworld travelers the worlds, realms or planes can have various levels, depending on the individual and/or their teachers and their own explorations.

Hedge witches do not roam the other realms for the sheer fun of it or the experience; we go there for a particular purpose whether that is for healing, spiritual advancement, wisdom, knowledge or for spell work. Therefore, only those who already have at least three years *intense* experience and study of witchcraft should attempt to hedge ride. That experience should cover all aspects of the Craft before attempting a journey. You should never hedge ride if you are ill, particularly if you have a mental illness as it can tip you into a psychotic episode, or leave you susceptible to negative entities. Please heed this warning. Hedge riding is not something to be undertaken lightly and without thought, by anyone inexperienced in the Craft or without some form of shamanic teaching. If in doubt, then go and seek teaching and only hedge ride in the company of an experienced rider or shamanic practitioner who can then guide and instruct you.

Before hedge riding, which I have been doing for twelve years, I had been astral projecting/travelling for thirty-nine years. Within astral travel, I have visited my own environment but also the three other realms, although for many years I did not know where in particular I was and just accepted it. This was a natural occurrence and it was not until I was a young adult that I learned to induce it. Anyone, who has the capabilities of astral projection, will almost certainly find it easier to hedge ride.

This book is not the definitive guide to hedge riding; it is simply a guide. The hedge riding aspect of hedge witchery is perhaps the most difficult part of the pathway. This book focuses on that aspect alone and further study, research and practice are essential.

If you want to learn more about Hedge Witchraft, there is an accompanying book in this series, *Pagans Portals — Hedge Witchcraft*.

I

What is Hedge Riding?

The 'hedge' in 'hedge witch' has more than one meaning. Primarily the hedge is the boundary separating this world and the otherworld. The hedge witch rides the hedge or as I like to say, has one foot over it, meaning she or he regularly explores the realms of the otherworld This is sometimes referred to as getting 'oot and aboot'. The hedge is also both psychically and physically protective keeping out unwanted visitors, spirit or human. It separates the witch from civilization, where she or he lives close to the wilderness on the margins of the town or village. In crossing the hedge, the witch enters the twilight, the veil between worlds, and emerges in the other realms, the lower, middle or upper.

Hedge riding is shamanic in nature and is related to *seidh*. Seidh which involves communication with the spirits, is often oracular, but does include other practices including magic and shapeshifting, which are also aspects of hedge riding. Modern seidh more often involves a group of people of whom one, the seer, is guided into trance (by one or more people through various methods such as chanting) and seeks answers which will serve the community or group. Hedge riding is usually solitary as the hedge witch is solitary, but there is nothing wrong in occasionally joining others for journeying and for support. Within a group, often the riders share symbols and even experiences, which indicates a psychic link can be formed within groups. Here though, we concentrate on solitary hedge riding.

When riding, the hedge rider's consciousness travels to another place, the otherworld, which is also the realm of the collective unconscious. There she or he encounters archetypal symbols and assimilates this knowledge to help guide her or him on their pathway.

I know this the tenth:
If I see the hedge-riders magically flying high,
I can make it so they go astray
Of their own skins, and of their own souls.
Nigel Pennick (Havamal, Complete Illustrated Guide to Runes, 2002)

A tenth I know, what time I see
House-riders flying on high;
So can I work, that wildly they go,
Showing their true shapes,
Hence to their own homes.
Henry Adams Bellows (*Hovamol, verse 156*, The Poetic Edda, 1936)

The above verses (two different translations of verse 156 of the Havamal) concern those that shapeshift (the witch) and who fly at night. Verses 147–165 of the Havamal are charms. Depending on which translation you follow, reciting the charm can cause either the hedge rider to show their true self and return home, or the rider's spirit to become separated from their physical body. *The Havamal* is from the Poetic Edda of the thirteenth century but perhaps composed earlier. The hedge rider of ancient times flew to the otherworld to consult with spirits and gods for the purposes of magic or prophecy. The hedge rider of modern times will certainly do this among other things.

As well as seidh, hedge riding has a kinship to what we

now call shamanism. Although indigenous peoples do not use this term and are more likely to use the terms 'medicine man' (or woman) or 'elder', for clarification I do use the words *shaman* and *shamanism*.

To gain an understanding of hedge riding, we first need to look briefly at shamanism in general. Shamanism is a generic term that covers a wide range of traditional practices and beliefs of indigenous peoples the world over. Shamanism, which is thought to have existed since prehistoric times, involves travel and communication within the spirit realms (often induced by drugs), and is used for divination purposes (as does Seidh), healing, acquiring knowledge, controlling of the weather and such things as exorcism.

Riding to the spirit realms is achieved by entering an altered state of consciousness (ASC), by such methods as drumming, drugs, fasting, dancing, and sweat lodges.

I will not insult these traditional people by comparing Western or Core Shamanism with the traditional. Traditional shamans earn their status having been 'chosen' — and often not through their own choice — having gone through some sort of hardship of pain or disease, such as mental illness, going out into the wilds for many days with no protection, food or water, or through suffering an NDE, near death experience (sometimes all three). They work with the darkness and with the light and live in harmony with nature. It is a lifetime commitment.

This is not to say that Western shamanism does not have its place. There are many good teachers of shamanism out there, but if you decide to take lessons to become a practitioner, it is best to investigate the credentials of the teacher first. Learning from an experienced practitioner can help you understand the spirit realms and your experiences there. You can then incorporate those teachings into your hedge riding practice.

So what is the difference between Western shamanism and hedge riding? In hedge riding, we do not usually practice psychopomp work, which involves escorting souls to the afterlife or work in a practice where people come to pay for healing or soul retrieval. Essentially, we practice from home and use hedge-riding journeys for healing, to search for knowledge, divination and for help in spell work.

As a hedge rider, I can only relate my own experiences of how hedge witches practice and others may work differently. As a spiritual seeker, I am still very much on a journey.

Straddling the hedge with one foot in either world is difficult (and not just because it sounds painful). Many people have problems passing into the otherworld without tuition. Others believe that when they pathwork this means they are accessing the realms, but sadly, this is not true. More often than not, it is just creative visualization, which they are inventing as they go. When you are truly hedge riding although your body is in this world, it is your spirit consciousness that is in the otherworld.

As hedge witches, we travel to the otherworld in an induced trance-like state or altered state of consciousness, achieved by various methods that suit us personally. The astral projection (AP) or out of body experiences (OBEs) I had experienced for more than fifty years (since a young child), helped me adapt to hedge riding. In more recent years, the visions and glimpses of the otherworld, the meeting of my animal guides many years ago, and the coming to me of passed away family members and pets while in an altered state of consciousness, progressed into hedge riding before I had even put a name to it.

However, it is not necessary to have experienced all these things to journey to the otherworld. It just needs fortitude and openness to experience, although a predisposition for psychic encounters, such as visions and lucid dreaming, does help.

Altered State of Consciousness

An ASC (altered state of consciousness) is a state that is accomplished by both natural and induced means, through which visionary messages are received and mystical experiences occur. In an ASC, your mind works differently than when you are fully awake in this everyday reality. Your mind and spirit is in essence separate from your body. With ASC, you are working just below the surface of full consciousness. This is opposed to the 'unconscious' in which things are hidden from you, so you are not conscious of them. In an ASC, we are always consciously aware of what we are doing. Drugs often induce this state though I do not use them myself. Steering away from drugs, there are much safer ways to achieve an ASC and that is through practicing meditation and moving onto visualization or pathworking with the aid of chanting, drumming or even listening to the beat of your own heart. Great concentration is required. From there further progression can be made. When you are in the otherworld, you know the difference from ordinary reality. You cannot control the scenery or what you see or who you meet.

In an ASC, we are lucid and able to control our movements, but we have to avoid falling asleep. ASC is similar to AP (astral projection) in that in doing so we dissociate our minds from our physical bodies. With me the AP is more often than not a natural occurrence, though is sometimes induced, while ASC is always deliberately induced in a particular and ritualistic setting.

To achieve an ASC it helps if you see yourself as an integral part of the universe. Everything is connected above and below, the planets, earth and everything on earth — everything seen and unseen.

To understand this better, let us compare it with synchronicity. Synchronicity is a concept of the psychologist Carl G. Jung. Synchronicity is a meaningful coincidence or a series of meaningful coincidences, with emphasis on 'meaningful'. It is when an outside event, or event of matter, coincides with a psychic or spiritual event, though in a meaningful way. Some of these events often contain archetypal symbols.

I was reading an excerpt from Maggie Hyde's book *Jung and Astrology*. In it she discusses how when writing the book she was talking to others about kingfishers and about how Jung found a dead one in his garden. No one at the dinner could recall anything about the habits of kingfishers. A few days later, she received a letter from one of the people at the dinner saying that the day after, he and his mother had seen a kingfisher over a lake and then the mother had told a story about finding a dead kingfisher five years before and had shown it to her granddaughter. The friend from the dinner could not recall seeing a kingfisher before. Maggie goes on to say that talking about kingfishers around reading Jung promotes this type of incident. In this case, two stories of a dead kingfisher and one live one came together in a synchronous moment.

By meaningful coincidence, after reading the article I went for a walk and stopped on the bridge over the River Fergus. I saw a kingfisher (the first I have seen in Ireland) fly along the fast flowing river. When it was out of sight, I turned to look over the other side of the bridge and the kingfisher flew back over the bridge and right in front of my face, causing me to jump back. It was so close I could feel the back draught from its wings.

This is a meaningful coincidence, although they might not always be as obvious as this one. By recognizing these synchronous events and acknowledging them and not just writing them off as coincidence, then we learn to accept that events do happen that cannot be explained. We learn that mind and matter, or the spiritual and matter (the seen and unseen), are just harmonizing aspects of the same reality and we are the connecting factor between the two events. And in this way we are the connecting factor between the worlds and between the conscious and unconscious mind. When we hedge ride, we cross the hedge, which is the veil between the worlds and we become the bridge or link between the two.

How to Achieve an ASC

There are several methods of achieving an altered state of consciousness, but perhaps the most popular is drumming.

A single drumbeat on a CD is the simplest, either record it yourself or buy or download a recording. If you have someone to drum for you then this is great. To begin with, keep it to twenty minutes. Most recordings have an ending after 15–20 minutes of several loud drumbeats to bring you back from your journey.

Music for shamans is also readily available. This usually has a mixture of music, rattles and drumbeats, and can be very effective.

Rattling before riding using a shaman rattle, can be quite effective in getting you in the right mind frame. Either sit and rattle or dance and rattle. Use it in combination with the drumming, and after a few minutes put the rattle down.

Dancing or Chanting before riding can also free up your mind ready for your journey.

Heartbeats have a rhythm like a drum. All you need to do with this is to sit in a quiet room and tune into them, wear earplugs if necessary. In fact, earplugs can help you hear your heartbeat better especially if your ear is pressed against a cushion.

I have used all of the above methods for journeying, sometimes one or two methods combined. I normally rattle and dance, then use either the single drumbeat or shaman music. However, it is what works best for you, and experimenting with different methods and combinations will help you find the way that suits you best.

Flying Mélange

Keeping a Hedge Journal

My *Hedge Journal,* is always at my side when hedge riding. As soon as I come out of my riding and am fully back in our own world, I record my journey. I cannot stress how important this is as you can forget details very quickly. Later if you try to recall them, you will be surprised at how many you have forgotten when you consult your Hedge Journal. You forget details of how your spirit guides look, or what they wore. If you did and saw many things on your riding, you will forget some of these. Even when you are writing, as you come down the page you will suddenly recall something you have missed writing about further up.

You can buy books such as those used for a Book of Shadows or Grimoire. Better still, make a book (or buy something plain) and decorate it yourself with items such as leaves, ribbons, or feathers — be as creative as you like.

Besom

Perhaps the item most associated with witches is the besom. An element of air, today it is used for ritual cleansing, but it is also a symbol of flight to the otherworld, especially if greased with the flying ointment mentioned below. The besom also protects. In the Netherlands, you will often see a besom standing outside the front door of homes. This is to ward off negative entities.

I like to keep my besom close to me when hedge riding.

Rattle

The rattle is used for invoking power and causing changes in your energy field, helping it clear and energize. It also rids the area of any negative influences. You use it to attract the spirits to guide you on your journey. Healing is another purpose for the rattle and when shaking it you can call on spirit guides to help in the healing process.

Hagge Bag

Many medicine men/women have a medicine bundle or drawstring bag. In *Erik's Saga* the original of which was said to have been written in the thirteenth century and of which two versions are preserved, *Hauksbók* and *Skalholtbók*, there is a mention of Seidh practice. In this story, a priestess, a *Völva*, was said to carry among other things, a belt with a skin pouch containing magical items. I have something similar and affectionately call it my *Hagge Bag*. Over time, we often find things that are symbolic to us or they come to us in a special way. This could be a stone, feather, leaf, piece of bone, shell, bead, crystal, twig, or a lucky charm. We might consider these items magical or for protection, or we might believe an item was sent to us such as a white feather from a loved one who has passed away.

The bag could contain items to represent each of the elements, or you can put rune stones in it. I carry both Uruz and Ehwaz, which are significant to me as well as representing my animal guides.

Smudge the items with a white sage smudge stick if you feel it necessary, or draw them through frankincense smoke. Think of each item and what it means to you. Keep all the items wrapped in a large cloth if they are bulky or perhaps a drawstring bag if they are small. The cloth or the bag can be made out of something you own such as a scarf. Perhaps you have some material that means something to you or has been within your family for many years. If possible, the cloth or bag should be of natural material such as cotton, though some people use animal skins. Open the bag during ritual or at special times, for instance when you need something from it, such as healing energy. You should keep it private from others and never let any of the items touch the ground, except if they are lying on the cloth. You can start with one or two items and add to it over time.

In time, the Hagge Bag will become powerful to you personally. You might like to have your bundle on your lap when you hedge ride.

Smudge Stick

The smudge stick is essential for cleansing the room prior to hedge riding. The smudge stick is a bundle of cleansing herbs usually made from sage/white sage or sweet grass or a combination. Mugwort can also be used along with lavender. Bunches of herbs are tied together with thin string. When lit the smudge stick exudes smoke with which the witch cleanses her/himself and the room.

Small Cauldron

This is handy for burning flying incense in. Light a small piece of incense charcoal and place in the cauldron. Sprinkle with your flying herbs. Ensure you have adequate ventilation and that the incense does not irritate your airways.

Ragwort

Let warlocks grim an' wither'd hags,
Tell how wi' you, on ragweed nags,
They skim the muirs an' dizzy crags,
Wi' wicked speed...
Robert Burns

In folklore, witches and faeries used ragwort stems as methods of flight. Although poisonous to cattle and horses if swallowed in huge quantities, there is no harm in keeping a sprig. As with any herbs and oils, keep out of the reach of small children. I keep ragwort in my Hagge Bag and sometimes hold it when I hedge ride.

Flying Incense and Ointment

In past times, flying ointments were made from poisonous and often lethal substances, such as hemlock, deadly night-shade, foxglove and monkshood. In more enlightened times it is wise to avoid these, as are drugs in general.

For deep visualization, hedge riding and trance, we can still use flying ointments and incense though these are in a symbolic way. As part of ritual preparation, this helps us get into the right frame of mind. I have found that the more you set your scene and prepare, the more successful astral riding can be.

You can make the following recipe into flying ointment

(using essential oils) or incense (using dried ingredients).

Flying Recipe

(You should use at least 5 of the ingredients)

Parsley
Poppy seeds
Mugwort
Sandalwood (use essential oil)
Jasmine
Wild Celery
Cinquefoil
Poplar leaf
*Silverweed

*For contact with nature spirits add Silverweed. I collect this every year when the silvery leaves appear on the ground. In making the incense, you actually use the roots, but if I pick it in the wild then I only pick flowers and leaves. The flowers appear in June. If I find it in my garden then I take some roots too. Faery folk are said to be partial to silverweed root.

For incense you should grind down the herbs with a mortar and pestle. Burn a few of the herbs on incense burning charcoal in a fireproof container and add a few drops of the sandalwood oil. The charcoal can be bought from New Age shops.

For ointment you should add 2 drops of each of the essential oils you have chosen to 50mls of sweet almond oil. Alternatively, you can use one part beeswax to two parts sweet almond oil. Place the beeswax and oil into heatproof bowl over a saucepan of hot water and melt. When it has cooled somewhat, add the essential oils and put into a sterilized jar. Keep it in the refrigerator. You can rub some of the ointment on your wrists, or onto the handle of your besom, which you keep to the side of you when travelling.

2

Learning to Pathwalk before You Run

Before attempting to hedge ride, if you are not experienced in meditation, visualization or pathworking, then you will run into difficulties achieving an ASC and will probably lack the skills to focus the attention. Here we will start right at the very beginning with some simple exercises to help you build some skills before moving onto hedge riding when you feel you are ready.

One thing most beginners have problems with is focusing the mind. If you are on a bus or train journey without anything to read, you might sit blindly staring out of the window thinking about various things; what to cook for dinner or who will win the match, or about work, school, your children, what you might be doing at the weekend or what you will wear for your night out.

When you are out walking, you can also easily find your mind wanders in the same way. This is called 'inner chatter' or 'inner dialogue'. However, you can teach yourself to keep focused by only thinking about what you are seeing, rather than what is happening in your life. Look at the trees, streams, wildflowers, and think about what you see. How does the wind feel on your skin? Do you smell the blossom of the trees? How does a birch leaf feel when you touch it? Every time your mind wanders to anything that is not to do with your walk, then bring it back to what you see, feel, touch, smell and hear.

The next exercise came from my friend another hedge witch, Kat.

Light a single candle and make yourself comfortable. Now stare at the flame of the candle. While staring, think only of the flame and what you see. If your mind wanders, gently bring it back to focus on the flame once more.

Before embarking on meditation, visualization and pathworking, you should be in good health, physically or mentally.

Meditation

Meditation helps you focus, organize the mind and shut out the world. It helps you achieve a peaceful and calm state of mind. Try this basic meditation:

Find a quiet room and a comfortable chair to sit on, or sit crossed-legged on the floor with hands loosely clasped. Ensure that every bit of your body is relaxed. Start with your toes and feet and release all the tension from them, then move up your legs to your hips and trunk, then your fingers, hands and arms, next are your shoulders, you will be surprised how stiff they can be even with the rest of you relaxed, then your neck, which can also become very tense. Lastly relax your face, your mouth, eyes and forehead. By concentrating on relaxing, you are already learning to stop your inner chatter. Keeping focused is difficult. If you have practiced the exercise of going for a walk or watching the candle flame and have managed to keep focused then you will find this easier.

Now with your eyes closed or half closed, concentrate on your breathing. Take notice of the breath in and the breath out and how that feels. Breathe naturally. If your mind wanders, bring it back to focus on your breathing. After a while, you should feel calm and peaceful. Do this for 10-15 minutes a day.

Visualization

Visualization or imagery meditation can simply mean picturing a scene in your mind and imagining something happening that you want, such as if you are ill, seeing yourself fit and well again. Or if you have mislaid an item, you retrace your steps to discover exactly when you had that item last and where it is likely to be.

As an exercise, a friend of mine found this useful. Find yourself a quiet room. Making sure you are not disturbed, seat yourself comfortably and close your eyes. Imagine you see an orange in your mind's eye. Look at the color of it, the texture and the smell. Turn it around, move it away from you and closer to you. Now imagine a triangle. It is red and is three-dimensional. Now turn it around and look at it from different angles. In this way, imagine more objects such as a cube, a globe or an apple.

If you follow the above exercises, they will help you form realistic images in your mind, and also help you focus.

Pathworking

Pathworking has come to have a variety of meanings. In general, pathworkings are visionary experiences and are the closest out of the three techniques to hedge riding, as often while pathworking you find yourself passing into the otherworld realms.

Pathworkings can be guided or self created. Guided (this is often called guided visualization or meditation), someone else talks you through what is happening and you visualize it and follow their instructions (this can be in person or through a CD).

The person who guides might do this to teach magical techniques, so you can gain a better understanding of symbols or magical methods.

I have also used it for healing and to guide groups to receive divinational messages. In this, everyone sits comfortably and the scene is set by darkening the room and lighting candles and incense. Each person will choose a rune without looking at it and hold it in their hand throughout the pathworking (you can use tarot cards and other forms of divination for this). I ask the percipients to close their eyes and relax every inch of their bodies. I then start the meditation music. I instruct everyone to breathe in through their noses and out through their mouths and be aware of every breath. I then guide them as follows. (This exercise differs slightly from one I use to teach connection with the runes.)

There is a door in front of you. It is a heavy oak door. Push this open and step through it to find yourself at the edge of a forest. There is pathway ahead… walk along this. Take in everything you see as you walk. Sunlight filters through the green-leaved trees. The bracken in the undergrowth is the color of jade. Beneath your feet are the remains of last autumn's russet leaves. The air is warm and a soft breeze gently ruffles your hair. The birds are singing their summer songs and you smell the wild flowers edging the path.

Ahead of you the path winds, but you do not see where it leads. In the distance, you can hear trickling water, but you cannot see from where. Look around you, what can you see — a bird? What kind of bird? A deer, or a rabbit, or possibly something not even connected with creatures of nature. Perhaps you see a flower, a person, a spectacular tree, or a nature spirit. There might be a mist swirling through the trees.

What about your other senses? Can you hear anything apart from the water, a bird calling, an animal growling, or a fire crackling? What can you smell? Musty, old leaves or smoke might assault your nostrils, or the beautiful scent of the wild rose floats past you. Touch the bark of a tree, feel its roughness. Is the ground hard or soft?

You continue along the path very aware of the rune in your hand. There is magic in the air. The path is widening in front of you and soon you meet the running water. It is a wide stream. The water is running faster and suddenly it drops down into a pretty waterfall. You decide to stop here. You follow the path downhill a little and you find yourself a big flat stone and sit down on it close to the waterfall. You watch as the blue damselflies dart back and forth over the water or a jeweled dragonfly whirs overhead.

You are again aware of the rune in your hand. Look around you. Is there a message in what you see? Is someone coming to speak to you? Look for narrative in the scene. Is a story unfolding that becomes a message? If you are compelled to do something such as swim, then do this. Now stay for a while...
When you are ready, retrace your steps and come back into the room, take a few deep breaths and open your eyes.

Once I have said, 'Now stay for a while...' I leave everyone to their own devices. After a few minutes, I continue by asking them to retrace their steps if I feel the pathworking is going on too long and people are not returning. When everyone has recovered, I ask them to look at their rune and write down what message they received. We then discuss what those messages mean to us personally, and how they can help us in our everyday lives. Some people are amazed at what they learn on the pathworking.

Sometimes, it is something that is prophesized and unfolds in the next day or so.

This is the lead up to hedge riding and is a journey into the unconscious to seek out archetypal images and their meanings.

To self-create a pathworking, plan first what you will do and then begin. When you emerge from the exercise you may well realize that you have not have been in control of some of what you did or saw.

You can use pathworkings to seek out a wise man or woman to ask for message, or look for symbols or books with written messages or for healing.

For healing, you could perhaps build yourself a temple within the pathworking. Again, I begin with a heavy oak door. This is so you familiarize yourself with one kind of entrance to the imagined world, and find it easier to progress from there.

You see a heavy oak door in front of you, open it and step though into a beautiful meadow. Walking through it, you push through the knee-high grass, which is dotted with the bright colors of cornflowers, knapweed, angelica and yarrow. Birds sing their early morning chorus and there is a refreshing summer breeze.

Ahead of you on the other side of the meadow is a grove of trees, in the center you see temple. The temple is made from white stone and is covered in green vine dripping with morning dew. A rainbow aura of color emanates from the temple roof, red, orange, yellow, green, blue, violet and indigo, each one has healing properties.

Approach the temple by climbing seven steps and enter it through the two Doric columns, which support the structure. The doorway is open and inside you can see the one room is lit with candles. In the center of the room stands an ornate fountain with three dolphins. Water pours from the mouth of one of them. On the rim of the fountain stands a chalice.

To the right of the fountain is a crystal clear pool of sparkling water. To the left there is a golden throne and above it is a rainbow funnel.

Now it is your choice whether to drink some healing fountain water, to bathe in the sparkling healing pool, or to sit on the golden throne and let the rainbow of color heal your whole body, mind and spirit.

Visit all three if you wish and spend a little time healing yourself. Feel the water, as you drink it from the chalice, run down into your body and healing you on the inside.

Bathe in the clear water and let it cleanse your mind of negative thoughts and emotions.

Sit on the throne and allow the rainbow funnel to cleanse each part of you starting with red at your feet and genitals, orange around the lower back and kidneys, yellow around the stomach area, green around the heart and chest and blue in the throat area. Indigo surrounds your forehead and will heal the brain area and enhance your psychic powers, while violet, which sits above your head will strengthen your spiritual links. When this is complete, a white light fills your body and radiates outwards.

When you are ready, retrace your steps and come back through the oak door.

3

The Three Worlds or Realms

The otherworld has three realms, which in themselves have levels. The lower realm for instance has an even lower level, the underworld. I access the three worlds through a tree, which stands close to the hedgerow. This tree is Yggdrasil or the *Axis Mundi*, a connection between our own world and the otherworld. For me it has three entrances, a portal in the roots, which leads to the lower world (the underworld I generally access via a passageway going downwards from the lower world), a portal in the trunk through which I access the middle world, and up in the branches a portal to the upper world (I climb the tree to reach this).

Although I follow a Celtic path (mainly as I live in Ireland and it is so much easier to connect with the local gods and goddesses), as you will see in this book I also have an interest in the Norse pantheon and mythology mainly through my use of the Elder Futhark runes, along with the belief my ancestors were Scandinavian as well as Irish. To read more about the runes please read my book, *The Spiritual Runes.*

Yggdrasil and the nine worlds actually correspond quite nicely with the three worlds, the upper, middle and lower, which I discuss below.

Yggdrasil the World Tree

In Norse Mythology, Yggdrasil is the world tree and is

usually accepted to be a gigantic ash. Yggdrasil connects all the nine worlds of Norse cosmology. The cosmology of the tree works together as one whole. All the different worlds are part of that whole. You will find the names of these worlds differ from source to source, so I use the ones most commonly mentioned and with modern spellings.

The worlds are on three different levels and it is not certain exactly how they are placed, so it is up to the individual to work out something that they believe is logical. This is my own version.

Asgard, *Alfheim* and *Vanaheim* rest on the branches of Yggdrasil in the upper world. Asgard is the home of the warlike gods the Aesir, ruled by Odin. Alfheim is the home of the light elves and ruled by Frey. Vanaheim is the home of the Vanir gods who are connected with nature and fertility. You can relate these three worlds with the upper realm.

Below these realms and connected to the upper world by Bifrost the Rainbow Bridge is *Midgard* which is the home of humanity, the land of men (as you will see in the journey examples at the end of the book I have also come across a bridge to the underworld while in the upper world). Midgard is surrounded by an ocean, which is the home of Jormungand the serpent. *Jotunheim* is the home of the Jotuns or frost giants and their stronghold which is called Utgard. It lies to the west of Midgard. Somewhere below lies *Svartalfheim*, the world of the dark elves or dwarves. These three worlds correspond with the middle realm. This world can be rather tricky and you can meet both positive and negative spirits there.

Muspelheim lies in the lower realms and is the home of the fire giants. *Niflheim* is a frozen wasteland, a land of ice and fog, and is ruled by the goddess Hel. These two lie in the upper level of the lower world, which is an earthy place and lies between Midgard and the underworld. The final realm in the lower world is the underworld realm of *Hel* or *Helheim*, which is the land of the dead (this is the lowest level). Hel is not to be confused with the Christian hell. It is the land of the ordinary dead (of those not killed nobly in battle). You can relate these three worlds with the lower realm.

Accordingly, the realms of the spiritual upper level are Asgard, Alfheim and Vanaheim, the realms of the Aesir gods of heaven, the light elves, and the Vanir gods of nature. These worlds represent the spiritual.

In the earthly level, things are more open and clear to us. It is the realm of humanity and of the practical, and materials things of our world, which we deal with every day. The realms of the earthly level are Midgard, Jotunheim and Svartalfheim, the realms of humankind, frost giants, and dark elves. These worlds represent the practical.

The realms of the lower level are Muspelheim, Niflheim the lands of fire, ice and fog, while Hel is the underworld. These worlds represent the unconscious.

The Lower World

The realm I visit the most is undoubtedly the lower realm, which exists close to our own world, so I begin with this. I enter this world through the roots of a tree. An earthy place of natural landscape and primal beauty, it resembles the earth as perhaps it would have been before the industrial revolution. This realm has almost any type of terrain and scenery and you will find forests, rivers, oceans, mountains, hills, valleys, dales, ice and snow, desert and jungle. Seasonal, it can be spring, winter, summer or autumn.

Animals, fish, birds and insects inhabit this world, and you will find squirrels, rabbits, hares, lions, tigers, snakes, lizards, dolphins, salmon, eagles, butterflies, dragonflies, bees, bears, wolves, deer and mice.

You will meet people here too, and my spirit guides sometimes visit though they dwell mainly in the upper world. I have also met one of my ancestors in this world along with wise men, goddess-like women, nature spirits and trooping faeries.

This realm is where I first met my animal guides and one of my spirit guides. I often visit this realm to look for guiding messages or simple answers to queries of my own or those of others. Here you meet with the archetypes of the collective unconscious.

Archetype is a word that was used by Jung to describe certain features of psychology especially in relation to the collective unconscious. Archetypes are symbolic images or motifs buried deep in the unconscious and which exist outside time and space. We share archetypes with all other people.

Jung studied Astrology, the I Ching, and Tarot, and many other ancient mysteries such as the Mandala. Archetypal examples would be such things as *the nurturing mother, the hero, the old hermit, the Divine child,* and *the young seductress,* which often appear in dreams and which he believed formed the basis of religion, myth, and art.

There are two sides to the unconscious, *the personal unconscious,* where we store things we do not need for now or things we want to forget, and the *collective unconscious,* which we share with everyone. The collective unconscious is like a reservoir of accumulated psychological inheritance that runs through all of humanity. Inherited from primitive times and through centuries past, it embraces all cultures. We share with other people these inherited archetypes and themes. They live on through us and are passed down to our descendants. It is a spiritual understanding.

The Vikings would agree with this view, as they believed the burdens of our ancestors are carried in our genes. Tapping into the unconscious can reveal our innermost hopes and fears. It is the bright side of life and the dark side of life. Jung calls these the *Anima* and *Animus*, which we must get in touch with along with the *Shadow* before we can truly get in touch with the *Self*. Getting in touch with the Anima/Animus can prove valuable as they can act as a messenger between the conscious and the unconscious, linking the two. For more on this read Jung's *Man and his Symbols*.

The lower realm is in my own opinion the easiest realm to access and I have visited it many times over the years both through astral projection and through hedge riding.

There is another realm, which you can access through the lower realm, though there are other ways, this is the underworld and a place of lost souls, and I tend to avoid it in hedge riding. Shamanic practitioners access this world during psychopomp work. I have visited there and in one journey, there was an underground river in a dark, impenetrable forest. In another, it was a great cavern.

The Middle World

A world I visit less than the upper or lower realms is the middle realm, and here I sometimes travel forward or backward in time. This world is like our own world though a spiritual aspect of it. When journeying there, you can end up anywhere, a house, city, country or in the countryside. Just as our own world is filled with dangers, this world can be too. Creatures and people you meet here can be tricky and you will find evil as well as good, so take care. I have come across demons here while astral travelling. The problem with astral travel is that you travel in a natural way and have less control of where you go. In the main, you also travel without dedicated purpose.

In hedge riding, it is best to avoid this realm if you are inexperienced unless you are travelling into your past (to visit the past you or perhaps your ancestors), or into your future (to meet the future you). Have this intent fully in your mind before riding there. Wait to visit it unless fully schooled in the way of the Craft and with riding experience of the lower and upper worlds. It could be that you wander in accidentally, but do not worry and follow the usual etiquette; there is a guide later in this book.

I access this realm through the trunk of my tree and I mainly go backwards in time and meet my ancestors. There is less danger that way. Here I have met more than once a young girl who appears to be Scandinavian. I first met her in the lower world and at that time, she brought with her Ox my first animal guide. I believe she is my ancestor and though I was actually looking to contact my Irish ancestors, she turned up. This led me to believe that my Irish ancestors have Scandinavian blood. Scandinavians often travelled to the part of Ireland from which my family origi-nates, settled there and integrated into the local population.

The Upper World

The upper realm, which I access through the branches of my tree, is a place of great beauty. Tropical islands, magical landscapes, landscapes of cloud and mists, of jungles and waterfalls, you will find here. This is where the spirits that exist on a higher vibration dwell. Here I have met my human spirit guides young and old, the wise ones, the gods and goddesses. These guides can appear in all guises: angelic, goddesses or gods, wise men and women, the old crone and Native Americans. Animals, fish, birds and insects also reside here and your animal guides will follow you there. Among the creatures I met in the upper world are eagles, deer, salmon, butterflies, herons, bees and snakes.

In the landscape, I have seen magnificent waterfalls, caves, mountains, bridges, ravines, white beaches, lakes and pools.

Accessing this realm though the branches of my tree, I then continue the journey on a boat via a stream, river or ocean. However, sometimes, I fly there.

I visit this realm for healing purposes, to gain wisdom and for knowledge. Scrying (skrying) is something I often do in this realm in dark pools of water, although sometimes my spirit guides give me runes or symbolic items.

Once, while in the upper world, I came upon a dark passageway in a cave, although I had entered many caves there, this one seemed dark and eerie, and I could see the passageway led downwards. I had inadvertently found a bridge from the upper world to the underworld, I did not want to go in and trusting my instincts stayed away.

Many years ago, in an astral projection journey, a young spirit child took me to the upper world and showed me around; this was my first journey there and it was a wonderful experience.

There are example journeys to all three worlds later in the book.

4

Animal and Spirit Guides

Animal Guides

We can see from the previous section that our animal guides play an important part in hedge riding. While hedge riding, it is advisable to have an accompanying animal guide (often called the power animal or companion animal). The animal guide can be a bird, a fish or a mammal, but generally it is a wild creature not a domesticated one. I have spoken to people who have had as a guide a mythological creature such as a unicorn. This does happen, however, it is not the norm.

I read once that you should choose your animal guide from one that is indigenous to your country or area so that you can meet with such an animal in real life should you wish to make a connection. However, with otherworld animal guides you do not choose them but rather, they have always been with you and they appear in the realms having previously been 'unseen' by you (except perhaps occasionally in dreams). So, although you might imagine that a wolf, bear, eagle or stag is your animal guide, you may well find it is a hare, turtle, or even an elephant.

After saying this, the animal guide does sometimes turn out to be an animal with which you feel a particular affinity or you may have had synchronous events that feature this animal.

You may connect animal companions with Native American traditions; however, animal totems have been around in many more cultures for centuries. The animal totem is a representation of a particular animal. Perhaps you do not have an animal companion and yet you have collected ornamental owls, horses or dolphins and have pictures of them on your walls. You feel a connection to this animal and seek them out in the wild, or in wildlife parks. You may have even written stories or painted pictures of this animal. Then in a riding, you find this animal is indeed your guide.

I personally was expecting a squirrel as a guide, but an Ox turned up and this was after accidentally passing into the lower realm when doing a pathworking and instead going into a deep trance. I first saw a young girl with blonde hair, which she wore in braids (this is the girl I now believe to be a Scandinavian ancestor). She had her arms around a large horned and white ox. I then became that girl. I could see the shine on the coat of the ox and feel its warmth. I belonged with it. Ox was truly my companion and felt I had a deep connection with him. Not surprisingly, he turned up on later hedge riding journeys. I walk with Ox or ride on him. Before I met Ox, I always carried (and still do) Uruz (the auroch) rune around with me. Apart from this, I have no connections with oxen.

Another of my guides and one that appears more often now is Horse, and I do have a special affinity with horses. I am a horse in Chinese Astrology and horses are associated with Libra, which I also am. Two years ago, there was a large mare with a foal down the road at a farm. I was told that this mare was unfriendly, rather wild and unapproachable. Each day I walked up to the gate and whispered softly to the mare. She would stare at me and appeared to be interested. On the third day, she came over to me and let me stroke her nose. She also let me pet her foal.

Some time ago, I was walking down the lane near my

home and a horse snorted on the other side of the hedge (this seemed significant and symbolic). He then started to gallop. I could hear him but could not see him. As I approached a gap in the hedge, I saw the horse pull to a stop. He was now ahead of me. He turned, looked at me, and nodded twice. He then began to approach me. There was a deep ditch separating us, but he climbed onto an embankment and then was as close as he could be. We looked at each other for several minutes, and periodically I whispered to him. The feeling of connection was wonderful.

I had a dream more than thirty years ago that I had to escape a terrible situation. It was one of those dreams rarely experienced more than two or three times in a lifetime. Often we have dreams that seem real and surprise us when we awaken, but this dream is one when it takes weeks to get over the fact that the dream was not your real life, it is that significant and has that much impact on you. In this dream, a nasty, horrid and ugly man wanted to marry me. I would be a prisoner for life.

I could not see what I looked like but could see that I was tall (which I am not), with long, thick, strawberry blonde hair and I was wearing a plain green wool dress. The man, who appeared to be an important person in the village, was with some of the villagers and they were saying that I was becoming a witch like my late mother (this seemed to be in a time that was after the so-called burning times) and that it was not decent for me to live alone after her death. Knowing they would not leave until I came, I said I would be out directly when I had fetched my things.

I walked back into the cottage where herbs hung from the rafters. I put on my cloak, went out though the back door and mounted a white horse, which stood outside, and rode off quietly over the hill. There was still much noise coming from the people and which muffled the hooves along with soft grass underfoot. When we were out of hearing range, we galloped along, it was raining and I was very wet, cold and tired. A long time later, the horse brought me to an old house and I dismounted and was able to knock on the door before collapsing on the doorstep rather ill. I was taken in and healed and the story went on and on.

Horse to me represents good companionship, relationships and partnerships, freedom, free spirit and spiritual journeys. We gallop along in the otherworld, the wind in my hair and me clutching to his mane. By coincidence, the second rune I carry around — and perhaps this is more a case of synchronicity — is Ehwaz the horse.

In the upper world, an eagle often appears to carry me to places. He picks me up in his talons. I also see an enormous snake periodically, and it appears always with Red Shirt (one of my spirit guides) when he is showing me knowledge. The last animal a white stag, which has accompanied me recently a few times, may well turn out to be another of my guides.

Your animal companion can run, walk, swim, or fly beside you. The guide is company for you so you do not feel alone. It will give you strength, confidence, and added protection. You might be able to communicate with it in some way but more often than not telepathically. You should also feel a deep connection with it, almost as if you are one being. The characteristics of your animal companion can transfer to you during your journey.

It seems then that everyone has animal guides throughout their lives but perhaps never gets to meet them, as they will never travel the realms. Animal guides can however appear in dreams and during astral projection.

To meet your guide, you need to be patient and open to meeting it. Using a shaman rattle before riding can encourage your animal guide to come to you. You will have no problem recognizing it as you will find that it will appear several times in successive journeys, or accompany you throughout a journey.

Spirit Guides

Spirit aides come in all shapes and forms and are an added form of protection and guidance in the otherworld. I have identified two spirit guides, one whom I met in the lower realm and one in the upper realm, both were men and the guide from the lower realm was older than the one from the upper realm.

The younger male guide I have seen only in the upper realm, while the older one I have seen in both the lower and upper realms. The older guide shows me wisdom and the younger one, knowledge.

It can take time to meet your spirit guides and they can appear in many guises. They appear several times, or in a significant way, that shows you they are there for you, to guide, protect and advise you. People wonder why their guides are often Native Americans or old bearded men in long white robes, it is a bit of a cliché, but guides often take a form that is most comfortable for us. Hence, both my spirit guides are Native American, one is called Eagle's Feather and the other Red Shirt.

Eagle's Feather first appeared in a cloak of golden eagle feathers. He wrapped me up in the cloak and I felt safe. In later journeys, in the upper world an eagle often appears and carries me to the tops of mountains and others places. I feel the two might be connected, perhaps a shapeshifting guide. Eagle's Feather has long hair decorated with golden eagle feathers.

Red Shirt wears a red shirt familiar in the old American West. The shirt has buttons down both sides of the front of the shirt, such as cowboys would wear. He has long hair and often wears a war bonnet.

I find it interesting that my guides — animal and human — appear to be male. I have seen a female, more often in the lower world. She is surrounded in light and wears white, but I do not yet know if she is a personal guide.

In astral projection to the otherworld-upper realm, my spirit guide is a childlike ethereal being and in this case is a girl.

Most times when I meet my spirit guides I receive a message, this is more often than not a silent message done with gestures, or the guide shows me something or holds my hands and a feel I know what they are telling me.

People and Creatures of the Otherworld

You may not meet many people or creatures in the otherworld until you have completed many ridings. As you become familiar with the worlds, people begin to appear. I have seen troops of faeries and groups of people, Native Americans in both a tipi and sitting around a fire, the bearded old man with long white robes, the white goddess figure, a man on a horse and an imp. You may see almost anyone, from goddesses to gods to archetypal figures such as the hero, prince, princess, queen or king, witch or crone, wise men and women, the mother figure, grandfather or a even a child.

Creatures are most often wild animals such as squirrels or hares, birds, deer and snakes. There are also jungle animals such as tigers and lions; some people see bears and wolves.

Shapeshifting

Attempts to shapeshift should wait until you are more experienced in riding. Again, learn to walk before running. It is better to know the otherworld well, have connected with your spirit and animal guides, and be able to cross into the otherworld with ease and to have undergone many ridings, before undertaking shapeshifting.

As I mentioned above, I believe one of my spirit guides shapeshifts into an eagle. But you can also shapeshift yourself. If we go back to the Havamal poem, we see that the hedge rider travels in guise, and the spell of the poem reveals the true form of the rider. Riding in animal form is an added form of protection. It also helps you take on the characteristics of the chosen animal.

To do this you take on the form of the animal before entering the otherworld, it is not the easiest thing to do and takes great concentration.

Alternatively, whilst in the otherworld, if you need to crawl into a small space you can become a snake; or if your need to fly, an eagle; or if you need to leap some distance, you can become a squirrel or a monkey.

By taking the form of your animal guide, you can become closer to it.

Shapeshifting Exercise

This exercise helps you in shapeshifting in the otherworld in a chosen form.

Find yourself a room with plenty of space. Put some suitable New Age music on. Now dance freely around the room. You may feel a little silly doing this, but keep going and you soon get into the spirit of it. After a while, take on the form of an animal, perhaps even one of your guides.

While you move around the room, act as the animal would, if it is a buffalo, you will plod, run and stampede around the room, and you might lower your horns to the ground, or you might paw the ground. If you are a horse, you will trot or gallop around the room, feeling the freedom of running. If you take on the form of an eagle, with your arms spread out you will fly and soar around the room, or a rabbit will hop. Get into the spirit of your animal. How does your animal, feel? What characteristics does he have ... wiliness ... slyness ... courage? What does he see or hear? Use all your senses to 'experience' what it is like to be your animal.

5

Protection, Preparation, Purpose and Etiquette

As a hedge witch, I will cross the hedge to seek help from the spirits and elementals that reside there for healing, strength, spiritual enlightenment, protection, sometimes simply to look for messages or solutions to problems, and for help in spell work, and knowledge, but mostly to gain wisdom. For what is knowledge without wisdom? I would never cross the hedge for magical empowerment or for material gain for I believe you receive what you need, not what you want. Journeying can be for yourself or others. Hedge riding is an individual experience and riders work with their own animal and spirit guides and without an authoritative overseer. Each individual seeks to grasp the meaning of their own experiences, but can ask advice or opinions of others.

Protection

Many people advocate using protection for any otherworld travel, as there are both positive and negative entities on the other side of the hedge. We never know what we might meet there. Personally, I have had few negative experiences though this was over a long period of time, but it does help to know that I am protected.

One of the simplest methods of protection is the blue or golden pool of light generated from the solar plexus area and surrounding us like a force field in an oval or egg shape. We form this pool of light around us by visualizing it emanating from the solar plexus area just below the breastbone. As it spreads through and around us covering us completely, we deepen the color to strengthen it. Being aware of it keeps it in place. It will dissipate naturally in time if we do not mentally keep it there.

In addition, we can hold an amulet of protection or wear one. I often hold a rowan twig or protective crystal loosely in my hand but I am also mentally aware of it.

We can shapeshift as an animal of the land, sea or sky. This would be an added form of protection rather than the only form, as animals are also prone to predators.

The best protection of all is your accompanying power animal or spirit guide. If you have not met your animal guide/s then your first journeys should be to achieve this. If you are not sure which animal it is that is actually your guide then ask that your guides be with you at the start of your journey even if you cannot see them.

Preparation

Scene setting is important to help you gain the correct frame of mind. Comfort is essential to aid concentration and minimize distractions. You will require peace and quiet away from noise and people and do make sure the room is warm, but not too hot. Use a blanket if necessary. If you prepare the setting an hour or so beforehand, you will ensure you have everything you need; there is nothing worse than distractions.

Light some homemade incense that is helpful for concentration and psychic work or use a non-toxic flying ointment (both symbolic), or smudge the room.

I often hold a quartz crystal, symbolic of seeing beyond the beyond, a natural wood wand, and a small branch of rowan or another plant I might have collected from the garden or neighboring countryside. I tend to keep smaller items in my Hagge Bag and leave it open on my lap.

You might like to buy or make a shaman rattle and use this first to invite your guides to travel with you. Rattle for a few minutes, though you may feel a chant coming into your head and if so sing it.

Play a drumming CD, or anything that will help induce a trance-like state. If you have a drumming CD, choose one of about twenty minutes to begin with and one with louder beats at the end to signal you to come back. With more practice, this can be extended. Alternatively, chant your favorite mantra or one you have put together yourself for the purpose. Drumming and rattling really are the best methods of inducing trance.

Wear earplugs if necessary to exclude everyday sounds (turning up the volume of the drumming to compensate).

Position yourself comfortably by sitting, semi-reclining or lying in a room with subdued lighting, preferably candlelit. I have found a sitting or semi-reclining position best as I tend to fall asleep when lying down.

Grounding

If you are hedge riding on a regular basis then you will need to ground yourself. You can do this before and after rituals and pathworkings. Grounding beforehand helps you keep one foot firmly in this world. Grounding afterwards will rid you of excess or unwanted energies. It will also help you reconnect with your own world. We can often become caught up in otherworldly traveling, and it is good to literally come back down to earth.

A standard grounding ritual is to stand with your hands by your sides and think of your body as the trunk of a tree. Be aware of the earth beneath your feet even if it is some way down as you live in a high-rise apartment. Take some deep breaths to start.

Now starting from just above your head, concentrate on draining all negative thoughts and excess energies by imagining them moving downwards through your body relaxing as you go. When you reach the root or base chakra area, this is the area around the base of your spine and pelvis, imagine growing roots from this area, which will grow downwards from it and also from the tips of your fingers and soles of your feet through the floor and deep into the ground. Think of the root tendrils creeping through the soft soil past the earthworms and moles and deeper though the rock and even as far as liquid mantle to the earth's core. Let the excess energy and anything negative run down the roots as they grow deep into the ground. Feel yourself anchored solidly. Then slowly release the roots and bring them back up. After you have finished take some more deep breaths, bend down, and touch the ground to give thanks.

Another way of grounding yourself, weather permitting, is to take off your footwear and go outside and stand barefoot on the ground for a few minutes. Relax and be consciously aware of the ground or grass beneath your feet. Connect yourself to the earth and be consciously aware of it. Alternatively, simply go out and plant something, weed the garden or dig in the earth.

Purpose

When hedge riding, you should always have a purpose for the journey firmly planted in your mind before you begin. If this is a question you want answered, go over it several times. If you go seeking furtherment of your spiritual path, then concentrate on it fully before you go. Think of your spirit guides and ask them to appear on your riding and show you the way forward. Keep focused on the purpose as you journey. Below are some of the purposes you may have for hedge riding.

Divination

The exercise in the section called 'Pathworking' is a good example of hedge riding for divination purposes. Alternatively, you could for instance to look for a dark pool and scry in it to look for symbols and images. You could also ask your spirit guides to help you with such things as decision making, such as whether it will be productive to take another job, or to ask will you be able to sell your house and move. You can also ask questions for others. I visit all three realms for divinational purposes.

Healing

Healing is a good purpose for riding. You should always heal yourself before attempting to heal others. One thing I do is to self heal by bathing myself in a sacred pool, most often in the upper world; this can also be done to cleanse yourself of negative thoughts and feelings. For healing or protecting others, I ask my animal guides to connect with theirs to help them with their troubles. Or I may ask my animal guides to take me somewhere I can heal, such as to receive much needed energy from a grove of trees or the sun, to look for clues to what might be causing my illness and ways to overcome that. Healing can be for physical, mental trauma or emotional purposes. Do not hedge ride if you are suffering severe mental illness such as psychosis or clinical depression or if you feel very unwell such as having the flu. People do journey when they suffer such illnesses as cancer as long as they feel well enough at the time, though a guided pathworking is perhaps more advisable. I have done this with a gravely ill friend of mine and she did gain much benefit from it in a spiritual way.

Spell Work

For spell work, my purpose might be to journey to the lower world for protection from psychic attack. The exercise might include asking my animal and spirit guides for the extra much needed protection, or to ask them why this is happening if I do not know. I also connect with nature spirits and ask for help in my purpose. I might look out for solutions, it could be that I see a thorn hedge in the shape of a circle and find my way to the middle, this image stays with me when I leave (I made this up as an example).

Spell work may include, gaining strength to see us through a tough time, or to look for ways to help us in our educational examinations. The purpose needs to be serious and not for trivial matters, such as wanting a designer handbag. Remember when riding for spell work that you reap what you sow, so do not go in looking for revenge, or anything that could be termed negative, because apart from attracting negative entities, there will be comeback for this.

Knowledge

I have sought knowledge in the other realms; this is spiritual knowledge and 'Self'-advancement. For this, I always journey to the upper world. My spirit guides have taken me to a cave where there was a large book; the book had messages for me. Another time my guides took me to see others, or to show me something. My guides hardly ever speak, and more often, I receive message through their actions in the most amazing ways. Often a large snake appears when I am to receive spiritual knowledge of some sort and accompanies or leads me to the place where I will find it. The snake appears to be a symbol of wisdom and is a guardian of the sacred places of knowledge.

Meeting the Ancestors

To meet my ancestors I travel to the middle world, but you may well meet ancestors in the other realms. As these are ancestors far in the past and that I have never met, the world is very different each time I go. Generally, I concentrate on which side of the family I want to meet, my maternal or my paternal side. This might be the Irish on my paternal side, or English and French on the maternal.

You can ask your ancestors for guidance in your life, or for words of wisdom.

Etiquette

There is a code of honor or etiquette that you should follow when meeting your animal and spirit guides, nature spirits or any other entities in the other realms.

The first and most obvious thing is politeness. Do not take your guides, whether spirit or animal, for granted. They are not your slaves to be there at your disposal nor is anyone else you might meet.

Normally the first creatures you meet on entering the other realms are your animal guides. Greet them on sight. Smile at them and spend time stroking or paying them attention before continuing on your journey. If you ride or fly on your guide, it is prudent to see if this is possible first. So ask them nicely. After a while, it may become second nature to mount your animal to travel more quickly and most are agreeable to this without having to request every time. The same goes for any other requests you make of them. When you say farewell to your animal guides, thank them for their protection and company.

With your spirit guides, you should also greet them and

give your thanks and say goodbye to them when you are ready to go. If they give you messages, take you anywhere, show you anything — again thank them. Never push for more than they can give. If you ask them something and they give a simple answer that you believe does not answer the question, still thank them and think more on it. The chances are that they have indeed answered your question in a simple way and it is up to you to figure out what that is or what it means to you. Always be grateful for the help you receive, and never take it for granted or presume on their generosity.

When meeting light entities (these are the gods and goddesses, helpful nature spirits and archetypal figures such as wise men and women, the child, hero, father, grandfather, wild woman, mother or crone), acknowledge them silently and wait for them to speak or show you what they have come there to do. When they have shown you something, led you somewhere, or told you something, thank them. Keep it simple. Nature spirits especially, prefer you to not be to profuse in your thanks. A sincere thank you will be sufficient.

Should you meet dark entities that you fear mean you harm, *will* them away. One way to help with this is to take with you a wand, have this on your lap and psychically conjure it up on the riding, should you need it. Touch away the entity with your wand. Alternatively have your besom nearby for the same purpose. You can also do this with a sprig of rowan or other protective plant, or in the case of nature spirits, something made of iron. Be strong of will and remove yourself from the vicinity and perhaps end the journey and return to your portal.

It could be that a spirit is very pleasant to you, is handsome, or beautiful. At first, you can be taken in by this. After a while if you become aware of something not right, the spirit trying to get into your mind for instance or you sense anything untoward, then again, will it away, or follow the steps above and return to your portal. Once you have done this and won over any negative entity, you will find them less likely to bother you again. But hopefully this will not happen to you, though it has happened to me.

6

Crossing the Hedge

Putting it all Together

Before hedge riding, set the scene, make yourself comfortable, and protect yourself; listening to drumming is perhaps the best way to start. When you feel ready, begin with a pathworking exercise of passing over or though a gap in the hedge. Alternatively, you can pass through a gateway, door or portal, which leads to the otherworld. This can be a cave, a hollow tree trunk, or the triad portal of trees, Oak, Ash and Whitethorn (Hawthorn). This should in turn lead into a tunnel portal, this is the twilight — the veil between the worlds. Continue walking along this or flying through the air. Then let the experience take over and hopefully you will pass into another reality by the time you emerge from it.

A friend of mine on her first journey, found herself riding an animal in the tunnel, which she soon came to realize was her animal guide. She remained in total darkness and never emerged from the tunnel. It was only on the second journey after some advice that she reached the end of the tunnel and discovered exactly what species her animal guide was.

Remaining in darkness can be caused by a blockage often caused by fear and self-doubt. In astral projection, I have occasionally encountered this too. You mentally block everything out. To conquer this, you need to lift the veil blocking out the images. You can do this by seeing a light up ahead and just emerging through it. The tunnel will be dark without some sort of light at the other end. Try not to doubt yourself, and just go with the flow and see what happens.

A tree is perhaps the best way to enter the other realms. The lower realms are accessed through the lower trunk and upper roots, the middle world straight through the trunk and upper world through the branches. Start by familiarizing yourself with the lower realm, before attempting to journey to the middle or upper realms.

Do not go with too much expectation. Have a purpose before you travel. Start by connecting with your animal guides in the lower world and then follow this up with something simple such as looking for a message. Someone might give this message to you, you might read it, or see it in the form of a symbol. As you become a little more experienced, you can try other things such as seeking healing, perhaps drinking from a sacred well, or cleansing through water, or meet someone who will offer you advice. You might not achieve passing into the otherworld for a long while but persevere. Even if you believe you have not put one foot over the hedge you might still have much to gain from this. You will know when you have been successful as you will have been totally immersed in this 'other' world, and the experience will be real. You will always stay aware that you are physically of this world, even though your mind is in the other.

Sample Journeys

The first journey you take into the other realms is one to meet your animal guides. One of the best places to do this is in the forest. Have this image firmly in your mind before riding the hedge. Also, use a rattle before you start, to call your guides to you. Dance and rattle or sit and rattle and mentally call to them. It could be when you emerge from your tunnel you are somewhere you did not expect. Look around you all the time and ask your guide or guides to appear to you.

Your guide needs to appear to you a few times before you can be sure it is particularly attached to you, so more than one journey will be required, though you can combine this with another purpose. It could be that you do not meet your guides the first time. In this case, do not worry but repeat the exercise on the next journey.

Below are some actual journey examples to help you understand what you may encounter.

Journey I (lower world)

I prepared the room, grounded and protected myself. Using the drumming CD, I started by standing in front of my tree, my portal to the otherworld, and passed through the lower trunk and roots, along the tunnel. Here I will describe the tunnel, but will not in the other journeys. Nor will I always add that I have greeted or thanked guides and so forth, so please take this for granted.

The tunnel was dark but there was a bright light at the far end so I could just see where I was going. The ground was covered with roots, as were the walls and roof. I clambered over the roots, watching where I stepped. Sometimes the tunnel seems endless. This riding was on one of those days so it took me a few minutes to reach the light.

I came out into a dense, dark forest. Ox my animal guide was there to greet me and I walked alongside him.

The forest looks different each time I enter it and this time it was rather eerie. There were many narrow tree trunks and the undergrowth was tangled. I kept seeing white tree trunks lying diagonally across the path. I mounted Ox and we travelled slowly at first but then as the pathway became clearer we picked up speed so we were rushing though the trees. At one point, we were a few feet off the ground. After a while, we stopped and I dismounted and sat on a log and watched the forest. I saw a man with dark hair and wearing a red tabard with coat of arms riding a dressed white horse. He kept coming in and out of my vision but never reached me. Next I saw a small standing stone, which turned into a grave headstone and the words 'peace', 'love' and 'live' appeared on it.

After some time, I again mounted Ox and we began to travel back as some time had passed. I saw a shiny axe standing against a tree but did not know what this was or why it was there. I did however believe it was more a symbol of productivity than of destruction or defense. When we see symbols they should mean something to us personally, and sometimes it is difficult to interpret them, and we might have to wait for another symbol to make thing clearer. Ahead I also saw the face of an imp in the trees. It did not look too friendly so I tried to touch it away with my wand but it persisted. As it did not move, I decided it was not threatening and continued. I dismounted at the hollow tree trunk and said goodbye and thank you to Ox and went into the portal.

Instead of emerging at the other side of the tree portal, I emerged directly into a something that resembled a Native American tipi. There were several men standing in it. They had long black hair, which was dressed with feathers. One of them handed me a pipe of peace. It had a long stem and was decorated with an intricate pattern. I felt I had been in the otherworld long enough, so I took a quick smoke of it to be polite and was about to leave when the powerful thought came to me that I could not smoke a pipe of peace by myself (this was another message). I waited patiently until all had smoked the pipe. This was done in silence. The men were not taking too much notice of me at this point so I quietly left the tipi and once more entered the portal and this time emerged where I had begun by the tree.

From this point, I found it exceedingly difficult to go from there back into the room. After some effort, about as much as I would use to leave my body in an astral projection or to wake myself up from a nightmare, I arrived safely back in the room.

The tipi experience was significant as it held a strong message for me.

Journey 2 (lower world: nature spirit riding)

With my purpose in mind, I entered through the tunnel in the roots of my tree and came out into a spring forest. Horse was there to greet me. I could see Ox in spirit form and I asked him if he could go to liaise with a family member's animal guides to ask for help and healing. He turned and drifted away.

Horse and I continued through the forest. Sometimes I rode on his back, and sometimes walked by his side. We eventually came to an orchard and the trees were in blossom. We walked through it and I could see a cave on the other side, I approached it, and saw it was dark and narrow. I immediately felt I did not want to go in and that it led to the underworld. I had been to the underworld before but had no wish to go to it at that point.

I retraced my steps back through the orchard and saw a white stag; this was the first of many sightings. He allowed me to approach and I stroked him and touched his great antlers and then continued onwards.

I eventually came to a stream. I paddled a little and found a hag stone. This is a small stone with a hole through it. I looked through it and saw a vision of my husband in a white shirt and he looked strong and handsome. I replaced the stone in the water (by coincidence not long after this a friend gave me a hag stone as a gift).

A small flying faery came towards me through the trees, as she came closer she suddenly grew to human size. She wore a shimmering white dress and had long blonde hair (I had seen this woman before in a vision).

As often happens to me with guides, she took my two hands in hers and passed over two items, one was a handful of soil, the other a paper with the word 'hope' on it (these items meant something to me personally). I thanked her and she walked away.

Continuing my journey, I came upon an enormous tree. One thick branch stretched out just above the ground and I lay down on it. The day was warm and beautiful, birds sang and the forest radiated with magic. I just lay and enjoyed being there.

After a while I heard some movement in the trees, I sat up and a troop of small faery folk travelled by. Some walked and some rode horses. They were about knee high. I decided to follow them and mounted Horse and we rode behind keeping a little distance. The faery folk rode into a large grassy mound, and I could feel myself being almost pulled in after them. It took much willpower to stay out of the mound. It was not that I felt danger, but as I did not know what would happen next, I thought it better to stay back. I mentally conjured up my rowan sprig and held it out in front of me and I was able to back away.

At this point, I had been riding long enough, so returned to my tree portal, said farewell to Horse and returned through the tunnel.

I had received messages that related to my purpose so was satisfied with the journey.

Journey 3 (middle world)
In this riding, I went through the middle of the trunk to meet my Irish ancestors, as I needed an answer to a question.

I emerged in a field; both horse and Ox were there. I walked for a while and came upon a young girl of about 14 years old. She wore good quality peasant clothing of a past time and I had met her before as she had introduced me to Ox. She was my great great (too many greats to put here) grandmother. I knew from before that she was Scandinavian. Then thoughts came to me that her family were immigrants, just as my own Irish great grandparents emigrated from Ireland first to New York and then back to Liverpool, UK. My family had always travelled in times of great need, just as the French side of the family had. The question I came to ask was answered.

I then had a strange vision of a pregnant belly, and the message that 'Where it is barren, there is seed'. This doubly answered my question (which was not about personal fertility).

I thanked my ancestor and my animal guides and returned. It was a short but fruitful journey.

Journey 4 (upper world)
My purpose for this riding was for divination. Using my shamanic music CD (rattling and drumming), I approached the upper world though the branches of my tree after climbing up. Again, it was through a tunnel. On the other side, I could feel magic and power; there was a river with a boat. It was in this boat that I sailed for some distance until I reached a lagoon. I stepped out of the boat onto the beach and took a path through the jungle. My two spirit guides Eagle's Feather and Red Shirt were waiting for me when I stepped into the clearing. There was a dark

pool of water, so I tried scrying into the murky depths but with no luck.

I went to the waterfall and river and crossed over by stepping across some large flat stones. I knew this area as I had been here before and I followed a pathway that I knew led to a cave. My spirit guides were not with me at this stage. A stone bench lay in the centre of the cave so I sat on this while I looked around. I saw a painting of a buffalo on the wall.

Going back outside Horse and Ox were there. I rode each of them in turn and they took me down to the beach. Here I ran around jumping and dancing barefoot in the sand. After while I left the beach and came upon another dark pool, there was something there but I could not work out what it was.

There was a bridge ahead so I crossed this. On the other side, a great golden eagle came down and picked me up in its talons (I have seen this eagle a few times and think it may be Eagle's Feather shapeshifting). I looked down as we rose into the sky and could see the boat below and a 'bird's eye' view of the scene; it was another message (I often get messages that are sayings or proverbs). As soon as I caught onto the message, he took me back down.

Red Shirt was waiting for me. He handed me three runes, Gebo (the gift), Thurisaz (the thorn) and Ehwaz (the horse). He also gave me an oyster shell. Another saying popped into my head, 'the world is my oyster'.

It was time to return, so I thanked him and went back to the boat and got in. I sailed back to the point of the tree and again felt great power and magic.

I was happy with this journey, as it had fulfilled its purpose.

Note

These journeys may seem short but some were up to an hour long. Many of my journeys have been very busy and I may have gone to a cave, bathed in water, climbed a mountain and many other manner of things in any one riding.

Persevere and try not be disappointed if little happens, for there will be other times that you will be exhausted from all the things you do and will find it hard to remember everything later.

Good luck with your riding.

Moon Books invites you to begin or deepen your encounter with Paganism, in all its rich, creative, flourishing forms.